A LITTLE HISTORY OF SCOTLAND

David Ross

Illustrations by Patrick Billington

APPLETREE PRESS

First published in 1995
by The Appletree Press Ltd,
19-21 Alfred Street, Belfast, BT2 8DL
Tel: +44 (0) 1232 243074
Fax:+44 (0) 1232 246756
email: frontdesk@appletree.ie

A Little History of Scotland

web site: www.irelandseye.com

A catalogue record for this book is available from the British Library

ISBN 0-86281-541-X

9 8 7 6 5 4 3 2

CONTENTS

ANCIENT SCOTLAND

Ten thousand years ago, Scotland had just ended its slow emergence from beneath a massive ice-sheet. The last Ice Age completed the seamed and rugged landscape we know today, though even now it is still rising from its long compression. The virgin soil was soon colonised by plants and animals, and man followed in their wake. The first inhabitants were hunter-gatherers with stone tools and weapons, who roamed the terrain for thousands of years. It was around five-thousand years ago that the farmers arrived, bringing skills and languages that originated East of the Mediterranean. They settled by the sea-shore or in lake-villages. Their kitchen middens and the remnants of their stone circles and buildings tell of people grouped in small communities, with a strong social order, a keen observation of the Sun and stars, and a strong sense of their place in the Universe.

No doubt these communities were always accustomed to pressure from incomers, from South, West and North-East. But in the centuries before Christ, the huge movement of the Celtic peoples westward through Europe reached its final stage here. Hill-forts still bear witness to the resistance they met. Aggressive, land-hungry, skilled in their own type of war, the Celts became dominant. But the fact that one of Scotland's peoples, the Picts, had two languages, one of them a Celtic type, the other related to no European tongue, suggests that the earlier inhabitants had been absorbed rather than wiped out: they have left their portion in the Scottish genetic cocktail.

Enterprising Greek travellers had sailed round Scotland, and explored in search of minerals, and tall stories about Ultima Thule were already being passed on. But Scotland enters the written record with the arrival of the Romans in the first century AD. Famously, they failed to subdue it, or considered it a profitless venture. The two walls, Hadrian's and Antonine's, remain to show the boundaries of the Empire. But the legions had been North at least to the Moray Firth, and in 84 AD, the Roman general Agricola defeated the massed tribesmen at the battle of Mons Graupius (Bennachie in Aberdeenshire). It was their war leader, Calgacus, who is quoted as saying of the invaders, "They make a desert and call it peace".

South of the Wall were provincial governors, paved roads, and a system of administration that reached back to Rome and even Constantinople. North of the Wall was Caledonia, with its shifting alliances of Celtic tribes, a warrior culture with bards to

Pictish carved stone

Skara Brae Village

recite their history and exploits, and stone carvers of a high order. The Roman conquest, when it came, was not a military but a religious one. In the fifth century, St Ninian established his church at Whithorn in Galloway; by the sixth, the great missionaries, Columba, Kentigern, Moluag, were at work, bringing the knowledge of Christianity from Ireland, founding monasteries out on the Western edge. For more than two centuries the tiny island of Iona was to be a centre of learning, of teaching, and of the splendidly intricate and decorative Celtic arts of carving and

Standing Stones, Callanish, Lewis

handwriting.

Ireland was also the source of the people called Scots, who settled in the West and carved out their own kingdom of Dalriada. Eventually, four distinct kingdoms emerged: Dalriada in the West, Pictland to the North, Strathclyde in the South-West (another Celtic kingdom, but speaking a language akin to Welsh rather than Gaelic), and Lothian in the South-East, with many speakers of Northumbrian English. A fifth element was added when the Viking raids began in the ninth century. Raiding was followed by settlement. By the early eleventh century the Norsemen were masters of Northern Scotland and the Western Isles.

Warfare and royal intermarriage blurred the boundaries. Kenneth McAlpin (died around 859) violently united the Picts and Scots and founded a vigorous dynasty which finally produced the first king to rule all these petty kingdoms and merge them into one: Duncan I (in 1034). But the North and the islands still belonged to the King of Norway.

At this time the entire population may have been around 200,000. It was still a Celtic society, inward-looking, its culture an oral one, the king a chief among chiefs. With ample fish, game and their black cattle, they had an adequate if predictable diet. Tribute would be paid in kind to chief and abbot, except for war service.

MEDIEVAL SCOTLAND

The facts of Scotland's geography have dictated the main themes of her history: a relatively infertile outer corner of civilised Europe; a small country sharing the same island with a larger neighbour; a country divided within itself into Highland and Lowland. From the 11th century on, these have controlled the development of the nation and all that goes with it by way of the national character, as seen from inside and out.

The first rulers of Scotland were Celtic kings of the house of McAlpin, maintaining a traditional style. But with the marriage of King Malcolm III to the Saxon princess Margaret in 1070, change began. She scorned the Celtic culture and the quirky Celtic Church which clung to its own traditions; she campaigned to make Scotland conform with the European states she knew. This trend was continued by her sons, who saw the advantages of the Norman feudal style of kingship, with its system of landholding in return for service, and the accompanying efficiency in many

St. Margaret

aspects of life from battle to business. There was a steady inflow of Normans, encouraged by successive kings. They built castles, established markets, set briskly about ensuring their own control of their allotted territory. For the first time, Scottish coins were minted, in the reign of David I, who became king in 1124. At this time (twelfth century) names such as Bruce, Fraser, Cumming, make their first appearance, with Norman incomers.

The kings used their Norman immigrants to help subdue such wild areas as the North East and the South West, with some success. Whilst the boundaries of the country were still undefined, they hoped to gain territory to the South, and also knew they must tackle Norway's possession of their backyard in the North. But it was easier to go South, and the pickings were richer. Northumberland, Cumberland and Westmorland had all been part of ancient Scottish kingdoms and the Scots kings made frequent attempts to assert their authority there. From William I on, the rulers of England threw them back. Indeed, even the Anglo-Saxon kings of England had claimed superiority over the Scottish king. The Scottish kings from David I onwards held earldoms in England and did homage for these; they all had to learn to live with the mixture of bullying and blandishment applied by their increasingly rich and powerful neighbour.

For all the difficulties of travel, the Norman world was always on the move. War, emigration, pilgrimage, trade all helped to set up regular communication and an increasing awareness of the known world. Master masons, trained in the most up-to-date style, came to Scotland to design and build great abbeys like Kelso and Dunfermline. Scotland sent emissaries to the courts of France, Burgundy and Norway, and the long alliance with France, the great counterweight to England, began.

Kelso Abbey

For a time, Scotland was a Gaelic-speaking kingdom. But the dynamic Norman newcomers, the Southern-oriented outlook of the kings, and the Northumbrian-English traditions of Lothian, where the king's principal seat was, encouraged the rapid spread of Scots English, and Gaelic began its long retreat. It was still supreme in the Highlands, and in Galloway, where the king's influence was slight except on his periodic "corrective" visits with an army recruited from rival earls. There was a lowland Scotland of castles, abbeys, farms and small market towns, where records were kept and money was used; and an upland Scotland of strongholds, huts, pastoral farming and hunting, where bards chanted the history and pedigree of the people and barter was the chief means of exchange. The hostility and misunderstanding between these two traditions is a tragic wound that runs through Scottish history.

Up to the late fifteenth century, conditions of life were gradually improving, and wealth and population increased. The Hebrides had been acquired from Norway, by purchase, in 1266, and only Orkney and Shetland remained outside the Scottish realm. The latter years of the 13th century became remembered as a "golden age" but this may have been because of the grim decades that followed it.

When, in 1286, King Alexander III's horse stumbled

and pitched him over a cliff at Kinghorn, Fife, his nearest heir was his infant grand-daughter, Margaret, princess of Norway. A committee of Guardians ruled in her name, but the child died, and thirteen men of royal descent claimed the throne. Edward I of England seized the opportunity to act as arbitrator, and eventually named John Balliol as king. But when Balliol showed some independence, Edward deposed and exiled him, and ruled Scotland as a military colony. He removed to London most of Scotland's historical records, and her most precious relic, the Stone of Destiny on which the kings had been crowned for hundreds of years. Resistance arose and reached a peak under William Wallace, who defeated an English army at Stirling Bridge. Edward softened his policy somewhat, but Wallace was betrayed, taken to London and barbarically executed. He had fought for Balliol as the legal king, but his successor, Robert Bruce, Earl of Carrick, led the struggle for independence in his own name as a claimant to the throne. In 1306, shortly after stabbing his chief rival to death in a church in Dumfries, he was crowned at Scone, the ancient centre of the Pictish kingdom. For some time his campaign seemed forlorn, but his own persistence (commemorated in the legend of "Bruce and the Spider") and the death of Edward I enabled him to establish his rule over most of the

Wallace Monument

country. The crucial battle came at Bannockburn in June 1314, when Edward II's attempt to reassert English control was shattered.

Under Robert I, a strong sense of nationality and patriotism developed, stirringly expressed in the Declaration of Arbroath, made to the Pope on Bruce's behalf by the Scots nobles and clergy in 1324 (he was still under excommunication for the 1306 killing). But the later fourteenth century was not a kind one for Scotland. Bruce's son David

II wasted much of his reign in war with England and consequent captivity. The first Stewart kings followed, descended from Bruce's daughter and Walter, High Steward of Scotland, but their rule was ineffective. Plague, border raids, local feuds and warfare were destructive in town and country. The country was at the mercy of such rapacious territorial warlords as the "Wolf of Badenoch" (King Robert III's own brother). Douglases and Percys fought their private wars across the Border, whatever their kings' policy might be.

As a boy, James I of Scotland had been sent to France for safety, but was captured by the English and spent his youth at the English court. He returned to Scotland in 1424 with a ransom to pay, and found a country where the barons were in control, with his uncle, the Duke of Albany, as the principal. But James had learned what was expected of a king, and his reign was to form a pattern for his successors: a child-king, helpless pawn of baronial power-politics, asserting himself in manhood and contriving to rule by managing the balance of power between his over-mighty and over-bearing subjects. The Douglases on the Border, the Macdonalds of the Isles, were broken. But in the Highlands the Campbells and Gordons rose in West and East to fill the vacuum of power. The successive Jameses, I to V,

Early Edinburgh

ruled vigorously (only the last of them died in his bed) and Scotland in the fifteenth century emerged from medieval twilight to join the community of European nations.

The kings' need for tax-money helped to promote the growth of commerce; their need to live in ostentatious luxury developed local skills and specialist trades. Palaces were built, or improved, in Edinburgh, Stirling, Falkland and Linlithgow. There was a Parliament, to make laws and raise taxes, with delegates from the "Three Estates": nobility, church and townspeople. The national spirit required the creation of other institutions. Universities were founded by energetic prelates such as Bishop Wardlaw of St Andrews (1412). The beginnings of an ordered system of Scottish law and the practice of scientific medicine can be found in the fifteenth century. By the early sixteenth century, small industries, coal mining, salt panning, were being developed, and with them an export trade across the North Sea. Greater wealth enabled the court and the rich to patronise poetry, music and drama, and these arts flourished. North of the Highland line, the chiefs maintained the culture of Gaeldom. But they too had to trade as well as raid, in order to acquire wine, and silverware, and weapons.

Real power in the country lay not with Parliament but with the king, the territorial barons like the Earls of Argyll

St. Andrews Students

or Mar, and the more able Church leaders. With her independence assured, Scotland developed a foreign policy, its prevailing trend anti-English, with crucial links to Denmark, the Low Countries, and of course France. The final territorial gain came in James III's reign, when Orkney and Shetland were pledged against the dowry of his wife, a Danish princess. It was never paid, and Scotland colonised the islands (1472). The French alliance, once a guarantee of national security, was seen as Scotland's great diplomatic lever. But in truth she was tied to it, and France held the handle. When France and England were at war, Scotland was expected to attack across the Border. The hazard of this was bloodily shown in the Battle of Flodden (1513) when James IV was killed with many of his army.

There were important long-term trends at work during the late fifteenth and early sixteenth centuries. Despite the French alliance, it was becoming clear, with the rising wealth and power of Tudor England, that Scotland's future would require some sort of accommodation with England at least in matters of trade. The church, which held a high proportion of the country's wealth, was increasingly corrupt, most of its high posts held by the nobility, its priests increasingly ill-trained and remote from the people. Fine churches were built and endowed, but the hunger for spiritual nourishment, and the visible scandal of infant royal bishops and priors, laid the ground for the doctrines of reform that were seeping in from England and the continent.

THE REFORMATION

In 1540, Scotland was a Catholic country, with a Catholic monarch and a Catholic population. In 1567, an infant Protestant king was thrust on to the throne of his Catholic mother by a victorious Protestant party assembled from all levels of society.

Many elements produced this change. Henry VIII of England noisily recommended his own version of Protestant reform and backed it up by invasion. Scots barons, ever-opportunistic, saw the possibility of church lands falling to them. There was a small but powerful merchant class whose education and knowledge of the world encouraged independence of mind. There was printing (the first press in Scotland was in 1507) and an urge to read the Bible at first hand. The Church hierarchy responded slowly and inadequately to the demands for reform. After the accession of Elizabeth I in England (1558) Catholicism also meant the continuation of French influence, and this had few benefits to offer. It would also seem that the Calvinist teachings

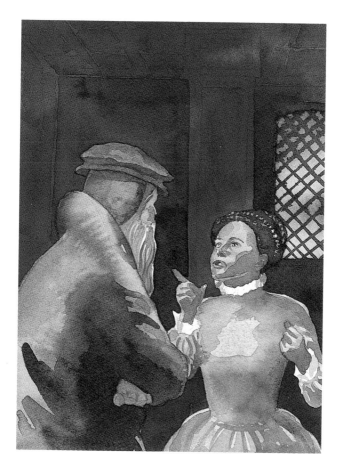

Mary Queen of Scots and John Knox

brought to Scotland in the 1550's by John Knox and his associates were very much to the public taste. It was a militant and stark creed that repudiated the past and proclaimed a direct relationship between the individual and God; and its new adherents were ready to fight for it. With English help, the French troops and advisers who helped to maintain the government of Mary of Guise (mother of Mary, Queen of Scots) were expelled in 1560. Protestantism was in control though the young Queen Mary, still in France whose Queen she also was, remained Catholic. In 1561 she returned, a teenage widow, to rule Scotland. Her deposition and flight to England, seven years later, had far more to do with her inept rule than with her religion. Her execution, for conspiracy, by the English in 1587, met with only a formal protest; her son, James VI, was the nearest heir of the childless Elizabeth I of England and had his eye fixed firmly on London.

By the end of the century, laws invented to keep down Protestantism were being used against Catholics. Priories and abbeys stood empty, their windows and statues long since smashed, their stones already being carried off. The vast wealth of the Church had gone to king and barons, with only a fraction being allowed to pass to its Presbyterian successor.

In 1603 Elizabeth I died, and Edinburgh saw her king depart to assume the throne of that neighbour which so often had been Scotland's bane, and often too a stimulus to progress. From then on, kings were absentees, but the country remained a separate sovereign state with her Parliament and her institutions all intact.

Scotland in Great Britain

Seventeenth Century

If any Scots thought that a shared king would bring economic rewards, they were wrong. The Border remained a customs barrier. Through the reigns of James VI and I, and his successors, the aspirations of Scottish merchants constantly grounded on the rocks of English obstruction. For their part, the English thought the Scots cheapjacks, selling low-grade goods at cut price, and spoiling the orderly working of the market, be it in cloth or hides, salt or soap. The Scottish pound always lagged in value behind the English one. While English merchants sold in bulk at their staple ports, Scottish pedlars tramped the roads of Northern Europe with their packs. Not for the only time, Scotland exported people. Scottish soldiers staffed the mercenary armies that swept Europe in the Thirty Years' War. From 1606, thousands of Lowland Scots settlers, full of the new doctrines of Calvinism, were given land and work in forfeited Irish estates in Ulster.

At home, religious dispute dominated the political scene.

Seventeenth-century soldier

Scotland had embraced Presbyterianism, which placed all ministers on the same level and made their General Assembly supreme. The kings wanted a "High" church governed by a hierarchy of bishops culminating in the monarch. In 1637, Charles I sought to impose a new liturgy, which led to rioting and to the drawing up of the National Covenant the following year. The Covenant demanded a free Parliament and a General Assembly, in a document which was essentially a declaration of rebellion against the king. War was inevitable, and the Covenant forces were victorious, capturing Newcastle. Charles was forced to make concessions. As his struggle with his English Parliament intensified, he came to Edinburgh in 1641 in a vain effort to win support there. In 1642 the English Civil War broke out. Both sides asked the Scots for help, but the sympathies of the church were with Parliament, and, for a price, Scotland entered the war against the king. The price was The Solemn League and Covenant, an agreement to reform the churches of England and Ireland along Scottish lines. For the Covenanters, it was a holy war.

Far behind their own lines, the Marquis of Montrose, once a Covenanter, marshalled a Highland/Irish army on behalf of the king, trounced the Covenanters in a series of brilliant victories, but at last was defeated. It had been a

Signing The Covenant

near thing, and the Covenanting army in England lost prestige. In 1646, his cause lost, Charles surrendered to the Scots at Newark in the English midlands; they held him for seven months and then handed him to Parliament, in return for some of the money they were owed.

When Charles I was executed (1649), Charles II was immediately proclaimed king in Edinburgh. He came to Scotland, then invaded England with an army that was routed at Worcester, and he fled to France. Cromwell invaded, defeated the Covenanting army at Dunbar in 1650, and once again Scotland was ruled as a military colony. The combination of the church's authority, down to the parish level, and the dictatorship of Cromwell, tamed the Scottish nobles more than any king had done. But repression also reduced trade, the occupying army had to be paid for: it was a hard time. The bitterest pill for the Presbyterian zealots was Cromwell's toleration of independent and breakaway Protestant sects.

With the restoration of Charles II in 1660, bishops came back. Scotland was ruled by a Privy Council which tried to balance the king's wishes against the temper of the people. The South-West had emerged as the home of extreme Presbyterianism and there were frequent disturbances there. Placatory efforts were followed by outright warfare.

Religion dominated seventeenth century life and politics, but the basic elements of life went on. In the style of the times, the Privy Councillors who formed the royal government sought to improve trade and line their own pockets at the same time. But Scotland, too small and poor to be a big import market, and dependent on exports, had little bargaining power, and most of her expansion of trade, across the Atlantic for example, was considered by the

Conventicle dispersed by Military

English as mere smuggling or even piracy. Individuals did work of great distinction in various fields, such as Napier's invention of logarithms (1614), Sir Thomas Urquhart's translations of Rabelais, and Viscount Stair's magisterial organisation of the law in his Institutes of the Law of Scotland, published in 1681.

James VII and II was an open Catholic and this provoked a Protestant rebellion by the Earl of Argyll, which failed, and much disturbance in the South-West. For a brief time, some prominent men turned Catholic to gain preferment; then James was deposed in England and fled to France. The Jacobite cause was born. William of Orange and his co-sovereign Mary, brought from Holland to replace James, were not popular in Scotland, despite their Stuart blood. They did abolish the Scottish bishoprics, but this owed more to the bishops' continued allegiance to James than to popular demand. Graham of Claverhouse ("Bonnie Dundee" to the Jacobites), who had fought down the Covenanters, raised an army for James, but was killed in the moment of victory at the Battle of Killiecrankie. The Catholic clan chiefs who had fought with him were compelled to take an oath of allegiance to William; Macdonald of Glencoe did so six days late and the Privy Council chose to make an example, the Massacre of Glencoe (1692) in which 38 people were slain.

The official barbarism of Glencoe discredited the government. As the seventeenth century drew near its end, the state of Scotland was not healthy. The small group of lords and notables who formed the government had no funds and no ideas. The country lived under the stern discipline of the church, enforced at parish level by humiliating punishments. This may have encouraged virtue and hard work, but also led to hypocrisy and evasion. Despite the church's aim to have a school in every parish, primitive beliefs and superstitions still abounded, and witch-burning was practised. Most people lived only a little above subsistence level, dependent on the annual harvest. In the pockets of industry, the workers were bondsmen, no better than serfs.

There were some signs of progress. Standards of living for the rich were improving, and beginning to spread downwards. Castles, which had mostly been little more than

Witch-Burning

Black Cattle Drive

fortified towers, now had great halls and spacious living rooms added. At this time, despite some lean years of failed harvests, the economy was diversifying. Glasgow was growing rapidly as a trading port with the New World. Tobacco and sugar were imported. Flax was grown to make linen. The old trades in cattle, fish, and hides continued. But the old constraints remained. To help counter these, in 1695, a trading company was set up, originally to trade with Africa and the Indies. It was ferociously opposed by English interests, who persuaded King William to forbid foreign investment in it. Eventually the company formed a trading colony in Darien on the Panama isthmus. It turned into a financial disaster that almost wrecked the Scottish economy, and caused intense anger and resentment.

Indeed, at the beginning of the eighteenth century relations between Scotland and England were as sour and hostile as they could be without actual war. The Scots, with a bankrupt economy, had few cards to play but one was the King. Queen Anne had no surviving children and the English Parliament had settled on the German (and Protestant) Hanoverians as her successors. The Scottish Parliament, with a strong Jacobite party, kept its options open. There was bitterness and tension in every area of trade and politics. It was a situation that could not continue. Against this stormy background, negotiations for a union of the two parliaments went on. The eventual proposals were intensely debated in the Scottish Parliament, while a hostile mob raged outside. But in April 1707, the Act of Union was passed, and Scotland ceased to be an independent nation.

Riot in Parliament

Bonnie Prince Charlie

SCOTLAND IN GREAT BRITAIN

Eighteenth Century

The eighteenth century was one of momentous change for Scotland. She entered it as a decrepit nation state. During it, she experienced the last violent eruptions of the ancient division between Highland and Lowland. Her capital, though shorn of political power, became for a time the intellectual centre of Europe. She ended it as one of the most technically advanced countries in the world, at the forefront of the Industrial Revolution.

With the Union, Scotland accepted the Hanoverian succession. She kept her separate law system, her church and other institutions. The Catholic and Jacobite elements, still substantial in the Highlands and the North-East, found surprising allies in the Presbyterians, who resented Westminster-made laws allowing local gentry to appoint ministers. Union had brought few rewards except to some highly-placed politicians. It was against a background of general discontent that the Earl of Mar raised the rebellion of 1715.

He mustered a large army, but it lacked effective leadership. "James VIII" appeared briefly and returned to France when the failure was obvious. The government saw that the Highlands had to be brought into line. The clans were ordered to disarm, but only those who supported the government actually did so; and General Wade was despatched to build roads and establish military control in the Grampians. Meanwhile, the consequences of union continued to create strains as Scottish trade and commercial tradition (including a traditionally corrupt excise system) were compelled to match English standards.

The central government faced an old dilemma in its treatment of the Highlands. Its Scottish predecessors had often relied on the power of the Campbells and their chief, the Earls, then Dukes, of Argyll, to keep order in the Highlands. The result had been to steadily enhance Argyll's power, and ensure that the clans threatened by Campbell expansion would remain hostile. Their continuing Catholicism and Stuart loyalty underlined this alienation. Even so, they were at first reluctant to join Prince Charles Edward, on his impetuous arrival in Moidart in July 1745. By September he was in Edinburgh and had defeated a government army at Prestonpans. But the mass of people remained passive. Nor was the Prince interested in Scotland only; the Stuarts would never abandon their claim to the English throne. He had to hazard an advance into England. As soon as he left Edinburgh the Hanoverian administration slipped back into place. Eventually, early in 1746, the Prince retreated into Scotland, having found no support in England. Despite a tactical victory at Falkirk, he was to meet final defeat by the Duke of Cumberland's army on Culloden Moor on April 16th. Highland clans fought on both sides, according to their political and religious adher-

Culloden Moor

ence, with broadsword and shield in a style that Calgacus might have recognised; the issue was determined by trained English and German musketeers.

The government now set about ensuring that the Jacobite clans would lose their taste for rebellion. The severity of their actions betrayed an attitude to the Highlanders not dissimilar to that which they would display to tribesmen in other countries. Gaelic society, the Gaelic language were now on the retreat even in their heartland. Chiefs became landowners, clansmen found themselves to be tenants.

The tragic adventure of the '45 was watched from the sidelines by most of the people. "Bonnie Prince Charlie" must have seemed a dream from the past come to life. They continued their daily activities of farming, commerce and industry. The prospect of improvement in many techniques, and access to vast new markets, drew the practical attention of many able people. An effective banking system was evolved, roads were improved, quality standards introduced into manufacturing, science brought to bear on agriculture. Considerable wealth was created and displayed in the "New Town" of Edinburgh and smaller developments in other towns like Perth, Elgin and Haddington. Scotsmen such as David Hume and Adam Smith radically changed philosophy and economics; the architect Robert Adam was defining a style that combined classicism, comfort and elegance; the artist Sir Henry Raeburn brought fresh life to the art of portraiture. Edinburgh society was confident and literary, but the two great writers of the time, Robert Burns and James Hogg, came from the small-scale farming country of the South-West and the Borders. And a generation of new men, engineers, was growing up. The work of James Watt, Thomas Telford and John Macadam, among many others, would transform society. The pace of change was accelerating.

Edinburgh New Town

Robert Burns

MODERN SCOTLAND

A curious change occurred in the century after 1746. The Highlands, seen before as an unattractive wilderness, inhabited by a barbaric, brutish folk, gradually became seen as romantic, beautiful, with people of heroic nature and splendid simplicity. This was largely because they had ceased to be a threat, but there were active agents as well. The first was James Macpherson, whose Ossian, and other "translations" from Gaelic brought him European fame in the 18th century. Even more influential was Sir Walter Scott. The phenomenal success of his verse romances and novels brought a new awareness of the vast rugged landscape and its people. The visit to Edinburgh of George IV in 1822 confirmed the new spirit. Tartans were devised, with elaborate notions of "Highland dress". But even as the beguiling legend of a Celtic Scotland spread abroad, the country was turning its central belt, where most of the people lived, into one of the most intensely industrialised areas in the world.

George IV

Cotton, coal and iron were the basis of Scottish industry. All required a large work-force, and population began to concentrate in Glasgow and the surrounding towns. At the beginning of the 19th century the population of Scotland was around 1,600,000; at the end of the century there were more than a million people in Glasgow alone. Inventions and improvements to inventions came faster and faster, a crucial one being the hot-blast furnace which could smelt the low-grade iron ore found in between the coal seams of Central Scotland. The new technology of steam power brought vast changes. To fill the demand for labour, many immigrants came from Ireland, still an agrarian economy; a substantial Catholic element appeared in the population. As the factories spread, and the mines went deeper, and the air became more sulphurous, social and political changes became clear. An urban working class was produced, used to living in close-packed streets, to the discipline of the steam-whistle, to a society equating betterment with material wealth. Workers had few rights; men, women and children laboured, often in dangerous conditions, for long hours, six days a week. Soon they perceived that they were the creators, not the spenders of the wealth, and political radicalism grew.

The rapid growth and concentration of population cre-

Steamship "Comet"

ated new social problems. Conditions in the crowded cities were atrocious. Hygiene was impossible, the diet was poor, and disease flourished. Local government had not adapted to the new conditions, there were few basic services, and reforms were made patchily through the early decades of the 19th century. Later, civic pride, new local tax systems, and private benefaction supplied museums, libraries, hospitals and parks. Fine town halls were added to, or replaced, the modest structures that had served unaltered since the 16th century.

Industry did not spread to the Highlands, which were not the unpeopled glens of today. There was a substantial population, widely if thinly spread. Their living standards were low. Peat was their fuel, oats and potatoes their staple diet, black cattle their source of income. On the west coast, they gathered and burned kelp to make alkali for the chemical industry. Their precarious economy was destroyed by the introduction of sheep farming, which needed plenty

Highland Clearances

of space and little labour. In the mid-1840s the potato crop failed. Emigration increasingly was the only answer; organising it for so many thousands became an industry in itself. When people were unwilling or unable to leave their homes, they were forced out in "Clearances" with varying degrees of brutality, leaving bitter memories. Scots settled all over the world, often, as if needing to replicate the peripheral position of their native land, in geographical extremities - the South Island of New Zealand, Newfoundland, Patagonia.

In the 19th century religion still was central to people's lives, but its old control waned in the cities. The controversies of the time were linked more to the Established Church's legal position than to matters of theology, but were still momentous. Opposition to the appointment of ministers by landowners, rather than by the congregation, led to the Disruption of 1843, when hundreds of ministers and congregations left to form the Free Church of Scotland. In parishes throughout the country a new church was built, and a new house for the minister, who also had to be paid. It was a stupendous effort.

Britain in the late 19th century was an imperial power and Scotland took full part in the operations of empire. Scottish regiments went to India, Egypt, the Crimea, South

Forth Railway Bridge

Africa. Clyde-built steamers ranged the world with Scottish-made products from locomotives and sewing-machines to whisky and cigarettes. Young Scots went out to tropical regions to run rubber plantations and teak forests. Glasgow proclaimed itself "Second City of the Empire" and celebrated its status with many fine Victorian buildings. There were pockets of dissent. The progress of Irish nationalism was observed, but politics in Scotland had already aligned themselves on Westminster's Tory/Liberal lines, and there was virtually no national movement. Unrest rose in the North-West in the 1880s, in the "Crofters' War" when small tenants set out to defend their rights, eventually secured in 1886. But the pattern of depopulation in the Highlands and Islands continued, and despite the taste for Celtic nostalgia, Gaelic was discouraged in schools. Sporting estates became fashionable, and vast areas of land were devoted to deer-stalking and grouse-shooting.

The story of Scotland in the twentieth century is essentially that of a province of Great Britain, sharing in the major events of the times - a fervent participation in the First World War, involuntary suffering in the Depression, industrial expansion as war loomed again, and five uncertain post-war decades in which spasms of economic growth

Glasgow School of Art

from new industry punctuated the steady decline of the coal- and steam-based industries. The people benefited from the improvements in social legislation, and while areas of the larger cities continued to be high in infant mortality, the improvement on the previous century was dramatic. As long ago as James II, edicts had been passed to discourage people from playing golf and football; archery was more useful. Now sport, amateur and professional, became part of everyday life, and in the case of the former, an impor-

Golfers at St. Andrews

Oil Rigs

tant source of foreign currency from golfers keen to visit the home of the game.

There are specifically Scottish themes: a leftward tendency politically is one. In the early years of the century, such Labour pioneers as Keir Hardie had also been nationalists; later the Labour Party became as unionist as the Tories had always been. Often, and most notably in the general election of 1992, Scotland would have had a Labour government whilst Great Britain had a Tory majority. The second half of the century also saw a strong recurrence of political nationalism. A referendum on limited self-government was held in 1979 and narrowly failed to meet the criterion of more than 40% of the entire electorate in favour. A further referendum in 1997 produced a large majority in favour of a Scottish Parliament with responsibility for virtually all internal affairs, and with the power to vary the levels of income tax set by the United Kingdom Government in London.

The renewed movement for a national government owes much to the history of the North Sea oilfields - an independent Scotland would have had a huge economic boost: as it was, Scotland's gains, though real, were limited. The profits went elsewhere, and a sense of lost opportunity remained. Although many nationalists opposed entry into the European Union, the existence of pan-European institutions has also given new life to the concept of Scotland as an independent unit within a wider European context.

Among Scottish artists, writers and musicians, there are those who consciously follow a Scottish tradition and those who defy such pigeon-holing. But the traditions remain; vibrant in the case of painting, renewed in poetry, still awaiting such renewal in the case of the novel. Gaelic, almost at its last gasp, has been given official support. Writers of great ability use it; along with Scotland's unique music, the pibroch, it may develop as well as survive.

Nearly three hundred years of political union have created all kinds of links between Scotland and England. Many Scots prefer to have the British rather than the Scottish stage to perform on. Argument goes on about whether Scotland pays into Great Britain more than she receives back (the Scotch whisky reserves are said to be of greater value than the bullion in the Bank of England).

Only the public will can determine these matters. What is undeniably true is that Scotland remains distinctively, proudly, sometimes defiantly, Scottish.

Some Dates in Scottish History

84	Battle of Mons Graupius
122	Building of Hadrian's Wall
563	Columba arrives on Iona
794	Norsemen pillage Iona
843	Scots and Picts United
1034	First unified kingdom
1266	Scotland gains the Hebrides
1314	Battle of Bannockburn
1412	First Scottish University, at St. Andrews
1472	Scotland gains Orkney and Shetland
1494	First mention of whisky in documents
1505	Beginnings of organised medical study in Edinburgh
1507	First printing press in Scotland
1513	Battle of Flodden
1603	Union of the Crowns
1603	First postal system in Scotland
1638	The National Covenant
1707	The Union of the Parliaments
1715	First Jacobite Rebellion
1722	Last witch-burning
1745	Landing of Prince Charles Edward
1746	Battle of Culloden
1749	First stage coach services, Glasgow to Edinburgh
1767	New Town of Edinburgh begun
1812	World's first working steamboat, on the River Clyde
1817	Founding of the Scotsman newspaper
1828	Hot blast iron smelting begins
1831	First steam railway in Scotland
1843	Disruption of the Church
1969	Development of North Sea oil fields
1979	First Referendum on Self-Government
1997	Second Referendum votes for a Scottish Parliament

Also published by Appletree Press

A Little Book of Scottish Verse
Compiled by David Ross

A Little Scottish Songbook

Scottish Toasts and Graces
Charles MacLean

The Little Book of Malt Whiskies
Derek Cooper

A Little Scottish Cookbook
Paul Harris

A Little Book of Clans and Tartans
Charles MacLean